Vienna

109 COLOUR PHOTOGRAPHS

A NUMERICAL PORTRAIT OF THE CITY

Vienna is the capital of the Republic of Austria and one of the 9 Federal Provinces. Third UNO city alongside New York and Geneva. 1.6 million inhabitants (some 20 % of the population of Austria). Area: 414 km^2. Altitude (city centre): 171 m. above sea level. 23 districts.
Approx. 60 km. from the Hungarian and Czechoslovakian borders.

2,000 YEARS OF HISTORY

A settlement area as from the Stone Age. A Celtic settlement several centuries before Christ. Foundation of the Roman military camp in the 1st cent. AD. Devastation during the *Völkerwanderung* in the 5th cent. First documentary mention of the name »Wenia« (origin unknown) in 881.
As from 1156 a Babenberg residence. Enlargement of the town. Civic rights 1221.
1278-1918 Habsburg rule.
Maximilian I's marriage policies bring a constant increase in power (». . . tu felix Austria, nube!«).
Development of a world-wide Empire of Spanish and Austrian Habsburgs.
(Charles V: »The sun never sets on my Empire«.)
Vienna becomes an imperial residence under Ferdinand I. First Turkish siege repelled in 1529. Rebuilding of the city fortifications as from 1531. Reformation and Counter-Reformation in the 16th cent.
Second Turkish siege 1683: relieved by Jan Sobieski of Poland and imperial auxiliary armies.
Prince Eugene again repels the Turks. Baroque heyday. Under Charles VI the Empire extends from the English Channel to Sicily in the south and to the Black Sea in the east.
Administrative, educational and social reforms in the reign of Maria Theresa (1740–80) and her son, Joseph II (1780–90).
1804 Proclamation of the »Hereditary Empire of Austria« by Francis I, 1806 dissolution of the Holy Roman Empire. Napoleonic Wars 1805 and 1809 (Archduke Charles' victory over Napoleon). 1814–15: the Congress of Vienna creates the basis of a lasting European peace.

In 1848, the Year of Revolutions, Francis Joseph I acceded to the throne, reigning until 1916. 1850 enlargement of the city, 1857 demolition of the city walls, development of the Ringstrasse, beginning of the »Gründerzeit«. 1869–75 regulation of the Danube: development of the Danube Canal and the Old Danube recreation area. In 1873, the year of the World Exhibition, economic recession due to stock exchange crash. The turn of the century was marked by a cultural and scientific heyday (art nouveau).
After the First World War (1914–18) Vienna had 2.2 million inhabitants.

In 1918 the city became the federal capital of the Republic of Austria. The Municipality of Vienna introduced internationally renowned social measures between the Wars: social housing programme (some 60,000 new apartments, exemplary health service and schooling).
Economic difficulties, social tension and a parliamentary crisis led to the civil war of February 1934, followed by the Austro-Fascist system under Dollfuss and Schuschnigg.

1938 Annexation by Hitler's Germany, Austria becomes the »Ostmark«.
In the Second World War (1939–45) roughly a quarter of Viennese buildings were damaged and 13 % were destroyed, among them valuable monuments.
1945 Arrival of Allied troops, reinstatement of the democratic constitution, proclamation of the 2nd Republic. Vienna is divided into zones of occupation (»4 men in a jeep«). Period of reconstruction.

1955: The State Treaty with the Allies restored full sovereignty to Austria. The constitutional act regarding perpetual neutrality was passed on 26 October 1955, now a National Holiday. In the same year Austria became a member of the UNO and the State Opera House and the Burgtheater were reopened.
A period of economic and cultural prosperity followed. Vienna became an international congress and conference city. In 1957 it became the seat of the International Atomic Energy Agency IAEA and in 1967 of the UNIDO. 1978: opening of the UNO City.

TIPS FOR VISITORS

SHOPPING: Elegant shops, boutiques, antique shops, etc. in the inner city (Kärntner Strasse, Graben, Kohlmarkt).

POPULAR SHOPPING STREETS:
Mariahilfer Strasse with large department stores (underground U3) and Favoritenstrasse (pedestrian zone, accessible via U1).
Shop opening hours: usually Mon–Fri, 8.30–18.30. Open until 17.00 on Saturdays.

EXCHANGE: Banks open Mon, Tues, Wed, Fri. from 8–12.30 and 13.30–15.00, Thurs. from 8–12.30 and 13.30–17.00. On Saturdays, Sundays and public holidays exchange facilities are available at the stations and at Vienna-Schwechat airport, automatic exchange machines in the city centre.

PUBLIC TRANSPORT: U-Bahn, S-Bahn (see last page but one) and a dense network of trams und buses. Reasonably priced tickets can be purchased in advance, day tickets, 3-day tickets, 8-day environment-conscious ticket (»Umweltkarte«) available at most tobacconists and underground stations. Single tickets purchased from the conductor are more expensive.

SIGHTSEEING: tours of the town by bus, hired car or on foot, for preference with a registered guide.
Constant service at the city guides centre.
Tel. 440 30 94

St. Stephen's Cathedral: the symbol of Vienna in the heart of the historic inner city, Romanesque and Gothic style.

Kärntner Strasse:
A shopping street of supreme elegance. Pedestrian zone.

Madonna of mercy and **Pilgram pulpit**, two of the loveliest Gothic masterpieces in the interior of the Cathedral.

Baroque main altar in the Cathedral of St. Stephen, showing the stoning of the Cathedral's patron saint. At the rear, Gothic stained glass windows.

St. Peter's Church: late baroque, consecrated 1733. Famous fresco in the dome.

Typically bowler-hatted **fiacre driver**.

Plague Column in the Graben, high baroque, built 1682–1693, dedicated to the Holy Trinity.

»**Anker Clock**« (1913–15) between houses no. 10 and 11 in the Hoher Markt. Daily at noon, a parade of historic figures with musical accompaniment.

Viennese coffee house, a world-famous institution.
Cafe Sacher

Specialities by the court confectioner »Demel« and . . .

the traditional Cafe Central in the Palais Ferstel.

State Opera House: one of the most famous opera houses in the world. Performances from the beginning of September to the end of June.

Opera Ball: a social highlight of the Carnival season in Vienna

Capuchin Vault: foundation stone laid in 1622, last resting place of the Habsburgs as from 1633

Double sarcophagus for Empress Maria Theresa and her husband, Francis Stephen of Lorraine, in the Capuchin vault.

Albertina: largest collection of graphic art and drawings in the world (Dürer, Rubens, etc.)
At the rear: the Hofburg and the Town Hall.
Right: the Augustinian Church.

Josefsplatz with the equestrian statue of Joseph II, Maria Theresa's eldest son and successor. Behind, the National Library.

Stateroom of the National Library. Largest library room in Europe, more than 2 million volumes. Collection of manuscripts, maps, music and globes.

»**Rothschild Prayer-Book**« from the National Library collection, dating back to c. 1510.

Michaelertor of the Hofburg.

Stallburg/Hofburg: Lipizzanermuseum

Spanish Riding School: top left, courbette; bottom left: classically correct strong trot; top right: school quadrille; bottom right: exercises on the long rein.

Schweizertor of the Hofburg: one of Vienna's few Renaissance monuments.
Passage to the Treasury and the Hofburg Chapel, where the **Vienna Boys' Choir** can be heard on Sundays.

Insignia of the Austrian Empire in the Treasury, originally made in Prague as the private insignia of Emperor Rudolf II and his brother, Emperor Matthias.

Imperial insignia in the Treasury:
Crown of the Holy Roman Empire, cross, orb and sword.

Emerald vessel in the Treasury. 2680 carat.
Cut by D. Miseroni, Prague, 1641.

Chain of office (Treasury) intended for the Herald of the Order of the Golden Fleece, founded in Burgundy in 1430.

Emperor Francis Joseph and his wife, **Empress Elizabeth**, known as Sisy. Painting by F.X. Winterhalter in the state apartments at the Hofburg.

State apartments in the Hofburg: the imperial table, laid according to Spanish court etiquette.

Emperor Francis Joseph memorial in the Burggarten.

Empress Elizabeth memorial in the Volksgarten.

Heldenplatz: Neue Burg. Main entrance to the National Library, the collections of arms and musical instruments and the Ephesus Museum. In the foreground, a fiacre.

Heldenplatz, **equestrian statue** of Archduke Charles, victor over Napoleon. At the rear, left, the Federal Chancellery and the Minorite Church, right, the wing that serves as official residence for the Federal President.

Prince Eugene memorial on the Heldenplatz. Austria's greatest general is mounted on his charger.

Kunsthistorisches Museum, harbouring the fourth largest gallery of paintings in the world (Bruegel, Titian, Velasquez, Raphael, etc.), a decorative art collection of note, an Egyptian-Oriental collection and antiquities. The Maria Theresa memorial stands in front.

Kunsthistorisches Museum, Portrait Gallery:
Raphael, »Madonna del Belvedere«

Velasquez: »Margarita Teresa in Pink«. The daughter of Philip IV of Spain later became Empress of Austria as the wife of Leopold I.

Pieter Bruegel the elder: »Return of the Hunters« or »Winter«. The Viennese Bruegel collection is the most extensive in the world.

The Museum Quarter in the former imperial equestrian stables is home to the Leopold Museum, the Museum of Modern Art, the Kunsthalle and numerous other art and cultural facilities. Picture, right: the Art History Museum and the Natural History Museum

The Leopold Museum houses the largest Egon Schiele collection in the world.
Picture: Egon Schiele, Self-portrait with physalis, 1912.

Parliament: built in the Greek style in 1874–83, ancient Greece being regarded as the mother of democracy.
In front of the building, Pallas Athene, the Greek goddess of wisdom.

Town Hall: built in the neo-Gothic style in 1872–83. Perched on the 97.3 m. tower is the »Rathausmann«, a symbol of Vienna. In the summer, concerts are held in the arcaded courtyard.

gtheater: 1874–88, The most traditional of German-speaking theatres.
gnificent staircase with frescos by Gustav and Ernst Klimt.

University: (1873–83), another typically monumental Ringstrasse edifice. Founded in 1365 by Rudolf IV, »the Founder«, the University of Vienna is the oldest in the German-speaking area today.

Votivkirche: (1865–79). Built in thanksgiving after an abortive assassination attempt on the life of Emperor Francis Joseph.

Sigmund Freud, the founder of psychoanalysis, lived in this house at Berggasse 19 from 1891 to 1938. The apartment and the consulting room are on view.

Strudelhofstiege: A masterpiece of architecture among the many flights of steps in hilly Vienna. Known on account of the novel of the same name by Heimito von Doderer, the Austrian author.

Griechenbeisl: Oldest restaurant in Vienna, Gothic tower. According to legend, this is where Augustin, a folk singer, composed the song »O du lieber Augustin«.

The Church of Maria am Gestade: one of the loveliest Gothic sacred buildings in Vienna. Now the Czechoslovakian national church.

The **Ruprechtskirche:** the oldest church in Vienna, said to have been founded in c. 740. Viewing only permitted before and after mass.

Post Office Savings Bank: Built 1904–1906 by Otto Wagner, a pioneering example of art nouveau architecture. Marble facade with 15,000 nails as a decorative element.

Sezession: Built 1897/98 by Josef Maria Olbrich as an exhibition site, it gave its name to Viennese art nouveau. Noteworthy: Gustav Klimt's Beethoven frieze.

»**Majolica House**«, Linke Wienzeile 40. Built 1898/99 as an apartment house by Otto Wagner.
Facade decoration of weatherproof majolica tiles. Beautiful staircase.

House in art nouveau style, Linke Wienzeile 38, also by Otto Wagner. Gilded medallions on the facade by Kolo Moser.

Karlsplatz Stadtbahn station by Otto Wagner.

Musikverein building. A centre of Viennese concert life of international repute.

Beethoven Memorial. The composer lived in Vienna for 35 years, creating most of his works here.

Golden Hall of the Musikverein.
Its acoustics are regarded as the best of any concert hall in the world.
This is the annual site of the New Year's Concert by the Vienna Philharmonic Orchestra.

Mozart Memorial in the Burggarten.

Memorial to Johann Strauss, the king of the waltz, in the Stadtpark.

Karlskirche. Vienna's most beautiful baroque church, dedicated (1737) to the patron saint of the plague whose life is depicted on both columns. Built by Fischer v. Erlach and commissioned by Emperor Charles VI in fulfilment of a vow at the end of the plague in 1713.

Schönbrunn Palace. Imperial summer residence. Building work commenced in 1692 with Versailles as a model, completed in the reign of Maria Theresa. The imperial apartments can be viewed throughout the year.

Empress Maria Theresa
State portrait in the hall of ceremonies at Schönbrunn Palace.

View of Schönbrunn Palace from the extensive grounds.

The **Great Gallery** in Schönbrunn Palace. For balls and receptions. Concerts are given here in the summer.

»**Millionenzimmer**«, Schönbrunn Palace. Ornately decorated wall panelling of an extremely rare wood.
60 gold-framed cartouches with 260 Persian-Indian miniatures.

Duke of Reichstadt. Portrait of the son of Napoleon and Maria Louise of Habsburg in the Palace of Schönbrunn where he died in 1832 at the age of 21.

The Duke of Reichstadt's **cradle**. A gift from the city of Paris to Marie Louise on the occasion of her son's birth, it is housed in the Treasury.

Coronation coach in the carriage museum at Schönbrunn.

Phaeton: carriage used by the Duke of Reichstadt as a child, a gift from his aunt, Caroline Murat.

Gloriette. Built in 1775 by Hetzendorf von Hohenberg as the culmination of the park. A monument to the Imperial Army.

Palm house in the grounds of Schönbrunn in the immediate vicinity of the zoological gardens.

Belvedere (= beautiful view), summer residence of Prince Eugene of Savoy (1663–1736). Built by Lukas v. Hildebrandt between 1714 and 1723.

View of Vienna from the Upper Belvedere. In the background, the chain of hills forming the Vienna Woods.

Upper Belvedere. The Austrian State Treaty was signed here in 1955.
It now houses the Austrian Gallery of 19th and 20th cent. art.
The Austrian Baroque Museum is located in the Lower Belvedere.

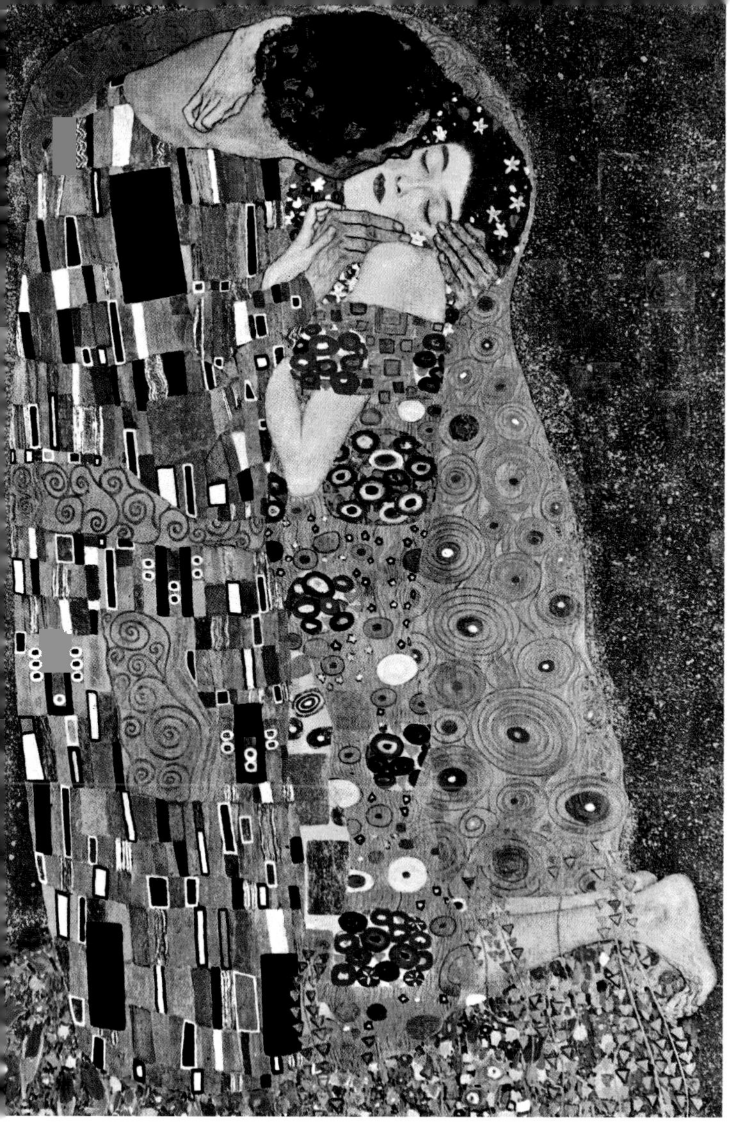

Gustav Klimt: The Kiss

Egon Schiele: Portrait of the danseuse Moa

Hundertwasser House: Built in 1983–85 as an experiment in communal housing, according to plans by Friedensreich Hundertwasser, the painter. 50 apartments, 13 green terraces, a restaurant and a cafe.

TELEPHONE

Red Army **Liberation Memorial** (1945) with, in front, the fountain erected to mark the completion of the first Viennese water conduit fed from high level springs (1873).

Danube Tower, built 1964. 252 m. high with panoramic terrace and slowly revolving restaurant. Superb view.

UNO City. Conference centre and Viennese seat of the United Nations.

View across the Danube to Kahlenberg and Leopoldsberg. The »Donauinsel«, created in the course of work on a flood barrier, is a popular recreation area for the Viennese.

View of Vienna from the Kahlenberg.
In 1683 **Jan Sobieski** and his troops set off from the Kahlenberg to relieve Vienna from the Turks with the aid of an imperial relief force.
Kahlenberg Church, consecrated (1783) in memory of Vienna's liberation from the Turks.

Prater: Imperial hunting grounds until 1766, opened to the public by Joseph II.
Part of the site is taken up by the »Wurstelprater« with its fun-fair and inns.
Built by English engineers in 1896/97, the giant wheel has become a symbol of Vienna.

Grinzing

District heating and incinerating plant Spittelau. Exterior design 1988–1992 by Friedensreich Hundertwasser whose multi-coloured painter's cap is reproduced on the building. The golden dome contains the control instruments for the measuring of the emissions. The district heating disposes of 250.000 tons of Viennas refuse and sewage per year in an ecologically friendly way.

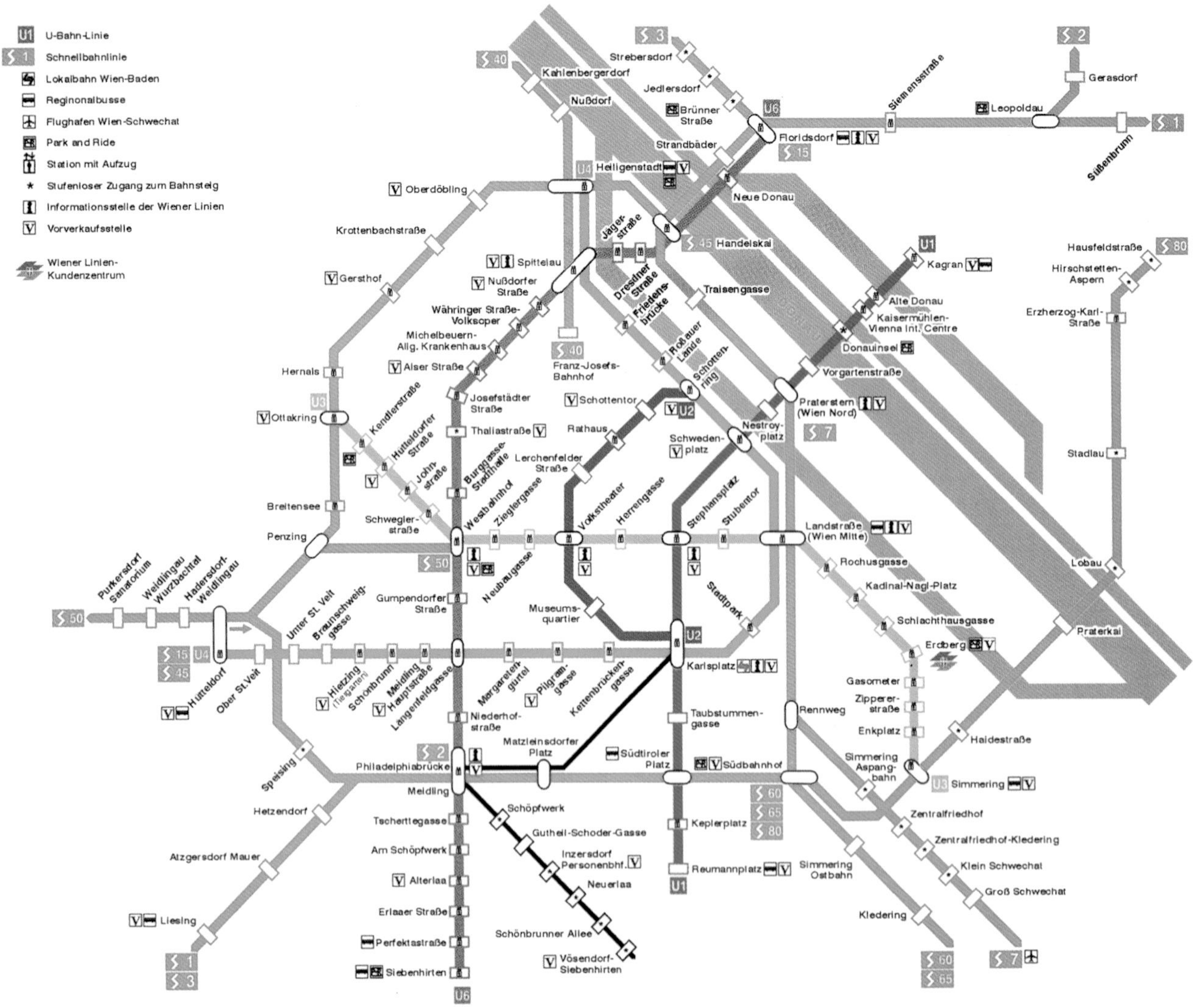
U1 U-Bahn-Linie
S 1 Schnellbahnlinie
Lokalbahn Wien-Baden
Regionalbusse
Flughafen Wien-Schwechat
Park and Ride
Station mit Aufzug
* Stufenloser Zugang zum Bahnsteig
Informationsstelle der Wiener Linien
V Vorverkaufsstelle
Wiener Linien-Kundenzentrum
S 3
S 40
S 2
S 1
Strebersdorf
Kahlenbergerdorf
Jedlersdorf
Siemensstraße
Gerasdorf
Nußdorf
Brünner Straße
Leopoldau
U6
Floridsdorf
S 15
Süßenbrunn
Strandbäder
U4
Heiligenstadt
Oberdöbling
Neue Donau
Krottenbachstraße
Jägerstraße
S 45
Handelskai
U1
Kagran
Hausfeldstraße
S 80
Spittelau
Hirschstetten-Aspern
Gersthof
Nußdorfer Straße
Dresdner Straße
Traisengasse
Währinger Straße-Volksoper
Friedensbrücke
Alte Donau
Kaisermühlen-Vienna Int. Centre
Erzherzog-Karl-Straße
Michelbeuern-Allg. Krankenhaus
Roßauer Lände
Donauinsel
Alser Straße
S 40
Franz-Josefs-Bahnhof
Schottenring
Vorgartenstraße
Hernals
Josefstädter Straße
Schottentor
U2
Praterstern (Wien Nord)
U3
Ottakring
Kendlerstraße
Rathaus
Nestroyplatz
Thaliastraße
Schwedenplatz
S 7
Hutteldorfer Straße
Burggasse-Stadthalle
Lerchenfelder Straße
Stadlau
Johnstraße
Westbahnhof
Zieglergasse
Volkstheater
Herrengasse
Stephansplatz
Stubentor
Breitensee
Schweglerstraße
Landstraße (Wien Mitte)
Penzing
S 50
Neubaugasse
Rochusgasse
Lobau
Purkersdorf Sanatorium
Weidlingau Wurzbachtal
Hadersdorf-Weidlingau
Kardinal-Nagl-Platz
Gumpendorfer Straße
Museumsquartier
Stadtpark
Unter St. Veit
Braunschweiggasse
Schlachthausgasse
S 50
Praterkai
U2
Erdberg
S 15
U4
S 45
Karlsplatz
Hietzing (Tiergarten)
Schönbrunn
Meidling Hauptstraße
Langenfeldgasse
Margaretengürtel
Pilgramgasse
Kettenbrückengasse
Gasometer
Hütteldorf
Ober St. Veit
Rennweg
Zippererstraße
Taubstummengasse
Niederhofstraße
Enkplatz
Haidestraße
Matzleinsdorfer Platz
Südtiroler Platz
Simmering Aspangbahn
S 2
Speising
Philadelphiabrücke
Südbahnhof
U3
Simmering
Meidling
Schöpfwerk
S 60
S 65
S 80
Zentralfriedhof
Hetzendorf
Tscherttegasse
Keplerplatz
Gutheil-Schoder-Gasse
Zentralfriedhof-Kledering
Am Schöpfwerk
Inzersdorf Personenbhf.
Atzgersdorf Mauer
Reumannplatz
Simmering Ostbahn
Klein Schwechat
U1
Alterlaa
Neuerlaa
Groß Schwechat
Erlaaer Straße
Kledering
Liesing
Schönbrunner Allee
Perfektastraße
Vösendorf-Siebenhirten
S 60
S 7
S 1
Siebenhirten
S 65
S 3
U6

Stand: 2.12.(